Sesquicentennial Collector Edition
The University of Missouri, Columbia • 1989

This book is a University of Missouri project from inception to completion. It is a time capsule of Mizzou on the 150th anniversary of the University. The Missouri Alumni Association sponsored the project; two members of the University of Missouri School of Journalism supplied the photography and designed the layout of the book; and Walsworth Publishing Company, Inc., of Marceline, Missouri, owned by two University of Missouri alumni, printed and published the completed work.

William F. Kuykendall

Bill Kuykendall is a member of the faculty at the University of Missouri School of Journalism. He directs the Photojournalism Sequence and the Missouri Photo Workshop. He previously worked in Seattle, Washington, as photography director at the *Seattle Times*. Kuykendall is an active member of the National Press Photographers Association. He was named Newspaper Picture Editor of the Year in 1970, served as editor in 1977 of that organization's official magazine, *News Photographer* and currently directs the University of Missouri NPPA Pictures of the Year competition. *Photojournalism/7*, a book compiled from the winning photographs of the 1981 Pictures of the Year contest, was edited and designed by Kuykendall.

David Rees

David Rees has taught photojournalism at the University of Missouri since 1986 and has directed the National College Photographer of the Year competition since 1987. He holds a Bachelors Degree from the University of Nebraska and a Masters Degree in Journalism from the University of Missouri. Previous to his positions in Columbia, Missouri, Rees was a sports writer for the *Lincoln Journal-Star* in Lincoln, Nebraska. He was employed at the *Columbia Daily Tribune* in Columbia, Missouri, from 1977 to 1986, where he was a photographer, director of photography, and photo and graphics editor.

David does freelance photography for regional and national publications, including *World Book Encyclopedia* and *USA Today*. He is the recipient of several awards for his photography and was first runner-up for the National Press Photographers Association's Region 7, Photographer of the Year in 1977.

Audrey Walsworth

Audrey Walsworth holds a degree in journalism from the University of Missouri. Audrey is an active supporter of the University of Missouri as a member of the University's Sesquicentennial Committee and president of the Gamma Phi Beta Corporation Board. She lives in Marceline and is active in community affairs such as the Community Chest. In 1988, Audrey wrote and produced a play for the centennial celebration of Marceline.

Don Walsworth

Don Walsworth is Chief Executive Officer and President of Walsworth Publishing Company, Inc., in Marceline, Missouri. He was graduated from the University of Missouri in 1957 and has maintained close ties to the University since.

Don has served on the University's Athletic Advisory Committee, the Medical School Outreach Committee, and the Business School Management Advisory Board. He is a co-contributor of the basketball locker room and media center at the school. His company is a corporate sponsor of the "Show Me Games," and the "University of Missouri Walsworth Classic Basketball Tournament." Don received the "University of Missouri Faculty Outstanding Alumni Award" in 1983 as well as being named the "Outstanding Greek Alumnus" that same year. Delta Tau Delta made him the first recipient of its "Man of the Year Award" in 1973. The Awards Committee of the University of Missouri Alumni Association unanimously selected Don as a recipient of the 1989 "Distinguished Service Award." This is one of the most prestigious awards an alumnus of the University can be granted.

Don has served as a civic and business leader, both locally and statewide. He was named Missouri Small Businessman of the Year in 1975, served as a director of the Missouri Chamber of Commerce, and is currently a Commissioner of the Missouri Highway and Transportation Department. He serves on the board of directors of several state and national corporations.

Bill Kuykendall

Audrey Walsworth

David Rees

Don Walsworth

Number 1852 *of 3,000 Limited Edition Copies*

Sesquicentennial Collector Edition
The University of Missouri, Columbia • 1989

This book is a University of Missouri project from inception to completion. It is a time capsule of Mizzou on the 150th anniversary of the University. The Missouri Alumni Association sponsored the project; two members of the University of Missouri School of Journalism supplied the photography and designed the layout of the book; and Walsworth Publishing Company, Inc., of Marceline, Missouri, owned by two University of Missouri alumni, printed and published the completed work.

William F. Kuykendall

Bill Kuykendall is a member of the faculty at the University of Missouri School of Journalism. He directs the Photojournalism Sequence and the Missouri Photo Workshop. He previously worked in Seattle, Washington, as photography director at the Seattle Times. Kuykendall is an active member of the National Press Photographers Association. He was named Newspaper Picture Editor of the Year in 1970, served as editor in 1977 of that organization's official magazine, News Photographer and currently directs the University of Missouri NPPA Pictures of the Year competition. Photojournalism/7, a book compiled from the winning photographs of the 1981 Pictures of the Year contest, was edited and designed by Kuykendall.

David Rees

David Rees has taught photojournalism at the University of Missouri since 1986 and has directed the National College Photographer of the Year competition since 1987. He holds a Bachelors Degree from the University of Nebraska and a Masters Degree in Journalism from the University of Missouri. Previous to his positions in Columbia, Missouri, Rees was a sports writer for the Lincoln Journal-Star in Lincoln, Nebraska. He was employed at the Columbia Daily Tribune in Columbia, Missouri, from 1977 to 1986, where he was a photographer, director of photography, and photo and graphics editor.

David does freelance photography for regional and national publications, including World Book Encyclopedia and USA Today. He is the recipient of several awards for his photography and was first runner-up for the National Press Photographers Association's Region 7, Photographer of the Year in 1977.

Audrey Walsworth

Audrey Walsworth holds a degree in journalism from the University of Missouri. Audrey is an active supporter of the University of Missouri as a member of the University's Sesquicentennial Committee and president of the Gamma Phi Beta Corporation Board. She lives in Marceline and is active in community affairs such as the Community Chest. In 1988, Audrey wrote and produced a play for the centennial celebration of Marceline.

Don Walsworth

Don Walsworth is Chief Executive Officer and President of Walsworth Publishing Company, Inc., in Marceline, Missouri. He was graduated from the University of Missouri in 1957 and has maintained close ties to the University since.

Don has served on the University's Athletic Advisory Committee, the Medical School Outreach Committee, and the Business School Management Advisory Board. He is a co-contributor of the basketball locker room and media center at the school. His company is a corporate sponsor of the "Show Me Games", and the "University of Missouri Walsworth Classic Basketball Tournament." Don received the "University of Missouri Faculty Outstanding Alumni Award," in 1983 as well as being named the "Outstanding Greek Alumnus," that same year. Delta Tau Delta made him the first recipient of its "Man of the Year Award," in 1973. The Awards Committee of the University of Missouri Alumni Association unanimously selected Don as a recipient of the 1989 "Distinguished Service Award." This is one of the most prestigious awards an alumnus of the University can be granted.

Don has served as a civic and business leader, both locally and statewide. He was named Missouri Small Businessman of the Year in 1975, served as a director of the Missouri Chamber of Commerce, and is currently a Commissioner of the Missouri Highway and Transportation Department. He serves on the board of directors of several state and national corporations.

Number ____ of 3,000 Limited Edition Copies

THE UNIVERSITY OF MISSOURI

150 YEARS

PHOTOGRAPHED BY DAVID REES

HISTORY BY AUDREY WALSWORTH

EDITED AND DESIGNED BY BILL KUYKENDALL

WALSWORTH PUBLISHING COMPANY

MARCELINE, MO

First edition printed in Summer, 1989 by Walsworth
Publishing Company, Marceline, MO 64658
816-376-3543

Hardcover International Standard Book Number:
0-940213-32-X

Special thanks: to Alumni Relations assistant director Mike
Kateman, '85; to MU journalism student and Alumni
Association board member Sidney Jackson; to University
Publications and Alumni Communications director Steve
Shinn, '50 and '71; to University of Missouri Archives
reference specialist D. J. Wade, '80; to Missouri State
Historical Society secretary Fae Sotham; to Walsworth
Publishing commercial sales manager David A. Schattgen;
and to all the University of Missouri faculty,
staff and students who helped make this project
so stimulating and rewarding.

THE UNIVERSITY OF MISSOURI WAS ESTABLISHED IN 1839, thanks to 900 Boone Countians who were the founding families. These were everyday people who dipped into their savings and mortgaged their homes so there would be a University and, most important for them, that it would be located in Columbia.

When Missouri was admitted to the Union in 1820, it was granted two townships for the establishment of a seminary of learning. In the 1830s, the legislature sold the land, and the proceeds were placed in a fund to endow a university. By 1839 that fund had grown to $100,000. The General Assembly then provided that the University of Missouri should be established and specified its location.

It was James S. Rollins, a representative from Boone County, who convinced the legislature that the University should be in the central part of the state, which would include Cooper, Cole and Saline counties on the south side of the Missouri River, and Howard, Boone and Callaway counties on the north. With competition in full force and with news that Callaway and Howard counties were amassing considerable pledges, Boone County increased the tempo of its campaign until 900 people had pledged $117,921.75 in cash and property. Thus the University was situated in Boone County.

Many across the state felt the University was just a Columbia institution because the members of the original Board of Curators were all from Boone County. In 1875, the Missouri State Constitution stipulated that no more than one curator could reside in a single congressional district.

From the very beginning there was a Board of Curators, even before there was a building or a president. Finally, in 1840, the University acquired a president, John Hiram Lathrop, and a building, Academic Hall.

In 1900, this institution of higher learning officially was declared the University of Missouri. The seal was adopted and the founding date of February 11, 1839, was established.

The University always has been plagued with money problems. At the outset, Missourians had little appreciation or understanding of higher education. The legislature did not appropriate funds for the University it had mandated, and interest on the seminary fund, which supported the University, was not always paid promptly. Often President Lathrop and the faculty went without pay. When the president's house burned in 1865, it was not rebuilt until 1867 because of a lack of funds.

The University survived on its own for 28 years before the General Assembly began supporting the school. It was Rollins again who stepped forward to aid the University when, as a legislator and a member of the Board of Curators, he proposed that the legislature appropriate the necessary funds.

A major storm was weathered in the 1860s, when the faculty set forth a plan to organize the University into departments, each with a professor in charge who would report directly to the Board. There would be no president, but a rotating

MISSOURI STATE HISTORICAL SOCIETY

Major James Rollins, a Boone County legislator, was influential in the decision to locate the University in the central part of the state. Boone County residents collected more than $100,000 and won the bid to locate the school in the county.

chairmanship of the faculty. The legislature reacted to the plan by dismissing the Board and the faculty. A new board was organized, and Benjamin Minor was appointed president.

Wars profoundly affect all aspects of society. The Civil War, combined with lack of funds, caused the school to close in March 1862. Federal troops were quartered in the main building, officers in the president's house and horses in the campus enclosure. The Normal (or teachers) School became a hospital. The University reopened in fall 1862, but the troops stayed, making normal functions of the University all but impossible.

The tenure of many early presidents ended for political reasons and often it took a long time to replace them. Several appointees were controversial, such as Samuel Laws, who convinced the legislature that the state would have to provide the money for necessary buildings because Boone County money had run out.

Richard Henry Jesse was inaugurated as president in 1891. Only 38 years of age at the time, he started a new era by enlarging the faculty, raising admission standards and developing the Graduate School.

MISSOURI STATE HISTORICAL SOCIETY

The 1875 campus included Academic Hall, the Normal Building, the president's house, an observatory and a lake.

On January 9, 1892, Academic Hall burned, destroying many books, furniture and paintings. The ruined walls were razed leaving nothing but the six Ionic columns that now symbolize the University. Although the main building was destroyed, classes continued without interruption, meeting in locations all over town. Taking advantage of this calamity, some other Missouri communities attempted to move the University out of Columbia. Once again, Boone County residents rallied and put $50,000 into the legislature's building fund to rebuild the University. They also filed a bond to guarantee the construction of an adequate water supply to prevent another such destructive tragedy.

The first residence hall was built in 1890 for 25 to 30 men. Before the Civil War, students boarded with townspeople. This was easily arranged because in 1868 there were only six students.

Additional buildings and dormitories started to spring up. In 1898, President Jesse had become concerned about discrimination against women students. Women boarded with townspeople for $4 a week when the University provided men's housing for $2. With expanding enrollment came more construction. Parker Memorial Hospital was opened in 1901.

Read Hall, a dormitory for women, was built in 1903. Whitten Hall was built about the same time. It was constructed of limestone, as Read Hall had been. The White Campus had begun. Enrollment was now around 2,000 and by 1912, the modern campus was in place.

On April 1, 1917, war was once again declared. Growth of the University came to a halt as students and faculty left for military service. Military training took the forefront, student social life dwindled and in 1918 the intercollegiate athletic program was discontinued. Later in the same year, the University had to be closed for three weeks as a result of an influenza epidemic.

During the early '20s the legislature was unusually generous with money, and several buildings were erected. Memorial Tower and Memorial Stadium were built to honor those students who had given their lives in the war. This spirit of generosity reversed in the later '20s, and appropriations dried up, although the general economy was good. This created quite a problem at a time of increasing enrollment.

Walter Williams became president just in time to face the Great Depression. To cut expenses he was forced to trim essential programs, dismiss faculty and cut salaries. Williams later resigned because of declining health.

Frederick A. Middlebush became president and his term was one of growth and improvement. Enrollment was increasing as were appropriations, which meant restoration of funds that had been previously cut. At this same time, the federal Works Progress Administration was created, bringing about one of the University's largest building programs. There were major additions campuswide.

The University, celebrating its 100th anniversary in 1939, had become secure at last in its position as a major university.

Then World War II intervened, and enrollment dropped from 5,000 to 1,500. ROTC and special military programs were expanded. The war was felt in all areas of University life, but this time sports went on as usual because the NCAA felt they were valuable morale boosters. At the end of the war, the flood of veterans taking advantage of the G.I. Bill of Rights changed the face of the campus. Anyone who had served in the war could afford college. Enrollment was back to 5,000 in 1945, and mushroomed to 11,000 in 1946.

Burgeoning enrollment put all kinds of pressure on the University. It expanded and operated with bulging seams, barely making do with limited instructors and facilities. Meanwhile, temporary buildings sprang up around the campus. The Board of Curators realized that, with such overwhelming needs, the legislature would not be able to appropriate enough funds. 1950 saw the start of paying for dormitories with bonds amortized through fees assessed against residents. Through-

out the '50s, '60s and '70s, additional enrollments made it necessary to continue building residence halls.

Another change took place when, in 1950, the first black students were admitted. Before then, Missouri supported the "Separate but Equal" policy. The state paid tuition and fees for blacks to attend out-of-state schools if courses they wished to pursue were not offered at Lincoln University in Jefferson City. Dr. Gus T. Ridgel, MA '51, became the first black graduate.

In 1953, KOMU-TV was started as a laboratory for television students, and in 1958 the Journalism School, in celebration of its fiftieth anniversary, established the Freedom of Information Center.

Failing health forced President Middlebush to resign and Elmer Ellis became president in 1955. Under Ellis, the University received $18.5 million in bond money and invested it in new buildings.

The Medical Center was created when the two-year medical college was expanded to a four-year program in 1951. The center was completed in 1960, and today MU boasts a first-class medical facility for patient care, clinical instruction and research.

The Memorial Student Union, after standing incomplete for 25 years, was finished in 1963.

In 1890, the University faculty sat for an informal portrait. The woman seated to the right is the chaperone for women students. It was customary at that time for women to sit apart from men.

When the Ag club chivaried "Prexy"

The Agriculture Club chivaries MU President Albert Ross Hill on his wedding night, ca. 1919-1920. Hill, who was 37 when he assumed the leadership of the University, was MIZZOU's youngest president.

Another major change that year was the establishment of campuses in St. Louis and Kansas City. A multi-campus university was relatively uncommon in American higher education at that time. President Elmer Ellis could see that it would be necessary for the University to expand to provide for the educational needs of students in St. Louis and Kansas City and that this could best be done at locations within those cities.

It also became obvious that Missouri would have to start depending on more private contributions. There has been a constant increase in this type of funding from $1 million in 1970 to $15 million in 1986-87. In 1988, alumnus Donald Reynolds, founder and CEO of the Donrey Media Corporation, donated $9 million for a new alumni center, MU's largest single gift to date.

When Herbert Schooling became chancellor in 1971, he appointed Walter Daniel vice chancellor, making him the first black administrator on campus.

In 1972 the Hearnes Multipurpose building was constructed, primarily for athletic events, but also for conventions, concerts and other special events.

In 1977, James C. Olson succeeded Brice Ratchford as president. Schooling retired and Barbara Uehling was appointed chancellor in 1978. She was the first woman to lead a major land-grant campus. During her tenure, University Hospital became fiscally sound.

Schooling and Uehling were great supporters of the arts and added much to the cultural life at the University by encouraging music, lectures and student theater. They also were responsible for much of the beautification on campus.

University cultural life had begun in 1842 with the formation of the two literary societies, the Union Literary and the Athenaean Society, which stimulated early intellectual life. The first department of Art was directed by George Caleb Bingham, the famous Missouri artist. The arts have flourished throughout all the changing eras. The University of Missouri, through its library and faculty, excells in the study of classical archaeology and art history.

The library is one of MU's most prized possessions. In 1858 its collection included 2,500 books. A recent $7.5 million expansion of the Elmer Ellis Library has made it Missouri's largest research library with 2.3 million volumes and subscriptions and more than 19,000 magazines and journals.

Throughout its history, the University has responded to the academic needs of the people of Missouri. As demand dictated, schools were founded and buildings built. The School of Mines was established at Rolla in 1870. Today it offers undergraduate and graduate degrees in arts and science, engineering and mines and metallurgy.

Women were admitted to the University in 1870 because there was a need for teachers. However, women could only attend the Normal School and were restricted to certain campus areas. They could only use the library and chapel at designated times.

To provide professional training, the Law School was established in 1872. It now has the 15th largest law library in the nation. In 1873, the two-year Medical School was established.

Missouri farmers needed specialized scientific training, and so the School of Agriculture was born in 1870. This school has been responsible for much of America's research into milk production and corn genetics. Work during post-war years led to the discovery of Aureomycin, an antibiotic useful in controlling a disease that threatened to wipe out the nation's bee colonies. The School of Agriculture brought Lespedeza and soybean production to Missouri. Barley and oats were improved, and hybrid corn was created with a cob that could be used for the manufacture of pipes. Pioneering work was done in wheat genetics.

The world's first journalism school was founded in 1908, with Walter Williams as its first dean. The J-School invented "the Missouri Method" of teaching which included intense practical training on the *University Missourian* which came

The University columns as seen from the dome of Academic Hall (now Jesse Hall) in 1912.
The photograph was taken by Volney McFadden, a student at the University from 1909 to 1914.

out on the first day of classes. From the beginning the paper was controversial. Williams set up a separate corporation to publish and protect it from University control. Journalism Week began in the second year and continues to this day.

In response to need, summer school began in 1898, and by 1908 extension courses were offered in eight areas around the state. The Graduate School began in 1910, and from the start received national recognition. The School of Commerce began in 1914 and grew rapidly. Later renamed the School of Business and Public Administration, it established the Bureau of Business and Economic Research.

In addition to academic programs, athletics have always played an important role in the life of the University. Intercollegiate programs date back to 1873 when MU played Westminster College in baseball. The first Missouri football game was against Washington University in St. Louis, in 1890; Mizzou lost 28-0. It was suggested then that the team be called the Tigers, a name given to a county vigilante group during the Civil War. The Missouri-Kansas game became the event of the year from 1891 on.

Athletic facilities expanded with Rothwell Gym, Rollins Field, A.L. Gustin Golf Course, tennis courts, handball and outdoor basketball courts. Brewer Fieldhouse was completed in 1930 and in its first year of use the Tigers won the conference title.

At the first conference football game, in 1929, the freshmen constructed the big stone M at the end of the stadium and made an annual ritual of whitewashing it.

Don Faurot took over the football program in 1934, winning two Big Six championships and playing in the Orange Bowl and the Sugar Bowl. Faurot returned after World War II to coach for seven more years, then became athletic director in 1956, and still serves the University in many capacities.

Faurot's successor as football coach, Frank Broyles, gave the first athletic scholarships to black athletes in 1956. Dan Devine succeeded Broyles and for the next 13 years had a most successful program, winning two conference championships and playing in six bowl games.

The football program suffered in later years and pressure forced the release of Devine's successors, Al Onofrio, Warren Powers and Woody Widenhofer. Mizzou's current coach Bob Stull will guide the Tigers for the first time in fall 1989.

Sparky Stalcup was head basketball coach from 1946 until 1962, and his teams won 186 games. In his 35 years as baseball coach Hi Simmons won one national championship and four straight conference titles in the early '60s. Not to be outdone, Tom Botts, head track coach, won eight conference championships and had a winning streak of 22 consecutive meets.

While the football program was suffering, the basketball side was succeeding handsomely. Norm Stewart and his teams won numerous conference championships, including a spectacular four-in-a-row with the team that included Steve Stipanovich and Jon Sundvold.

Women's sports have come into their own in recent years, especially basketball, golf, track and gymnastics.

Changes in student life have been recorded throughout the years in the University yearbook, *The Savitar*, first published in 1895. Today *The Savitar* is suffering through a period of financial and management problems, and its continued publication is in jeopardy.

In 1950, " Black Jack" Matthews was named to the newly created post of dean of students, and in late 1959, the Missouri Students Association was formed to speak for student rights. The MSA conducted anti-Vietnam War protests and also was responsible for increasing student participation in University affairs and the relaxation of some rules. In the '80s, students lobbied for, and won, a seat on the Board of Curators.

As for student activities, the fraternity-sorority system was at its peak in the '50s. Rush week was a time of hubbub and high expectations. Marching Mizzou

UNIVERSITY OF MISSOURI ARCHIVES

A member of the MU football team ca. 1914.

became a thrilling part of the football scene, having evolved from the cadet band of long ago. Homecoming has always revived memories of floats, house decorations and nominees for queen. But even Homecoming has undergone changes. The queen evolved to a king and queen in 1977. In 1985, for the first time in University history, a black couple presided over the Homecoming Court.

Many hours of social time have been spent at Hinkson Creek, Hulen's Lake, Andy's Corner and the Stables. The Shack is no longer a part of the University scene, having burned in the fall of 1988.

The *Maneater*, the controversial student newspaper, continues but *Showme*, the humor magazine of 40 years, ceased publication in 1964.

In this 150th year, in which C. Peter Magrath serves as president and Haskell Monroe as chancellor, there are many things of which to be proud. MU has pioneered in the utilization of computers to bring the University's scientific and technological capacity to communities throughout the state. Physicians statewide depend on University computers to make diagnoses. The University has received national acclaim for radiological computer research and can boast a research reactor five times more powerful than any other university reactor in the country. The College of Agriculture has provided national leadership in the transfer of agricultural techniques to underdeveloped countries.

Looking back over MU's 150 years, several themes stand out—the desire from the outset for quality, the constant fight to survive, the search for excellence and the commitment to fill the needs of people.

When adversity has struck, as with the loss of Academic Hall, the University has rebuilt better, bigger and quickly. MU's philosophy and entrance regulations have evolved to keep abreast of changing times and the state's needs. New teaching methods have been developed, using clinical and practical experience and state-of-the-art equipment. Despite the never-ending financial struggle, the Mizzou attitude has been to forge ahead and offer the state the best educational facility possible with the resources that are available.

With the coming years, we look forward to continued intellectual, scientific, physical and cultural growth that will maintain the reputation of the University of Missouri and its students, faculty, staff and alumni, as one of Missouri's greatest resources.

— **Audrey Walsworth, June, 1989**

For more about MIZZOU, read **The University of Missouri, an Illustrated History** by James and Vera Olson.

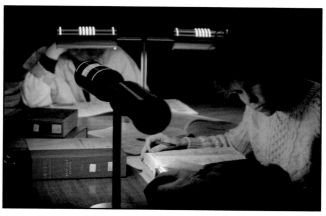

Walter Johnson lectures his Economics 51 class.

Music Professor Carleton Spotts, a member of the Esterhazy Quartet, practices his cello.

Victor Lambeth, professor of horticulture, is in charge of the tomato research program that has developed 40 marketable hybrids.

Sanborn Field, with its 100-year-old test plots, is unique in agriculture research.

Patrice Albert, research specialist in Biological Sciences, Tucker Hall.

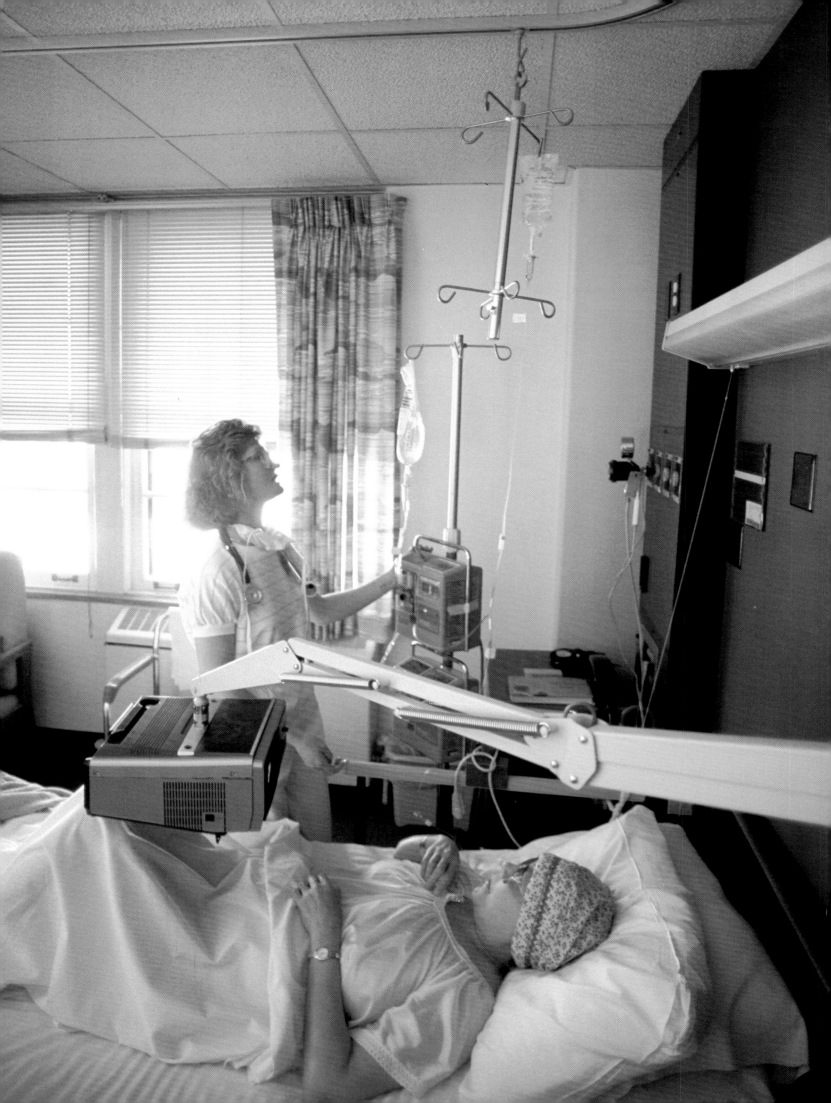

A student monitors a class in Trial Practice at the Law School.

Prof. H. Carl Gerhardt, Jr., has found that the voiceprint of tree frogs is as distinctive as their DNA.

Chancellor Haskell Monroe teaches a 7:40 a.m. class in American history.

English Prof. William "Mac" Jones is a recipient of the Purple Chalk teaching award.

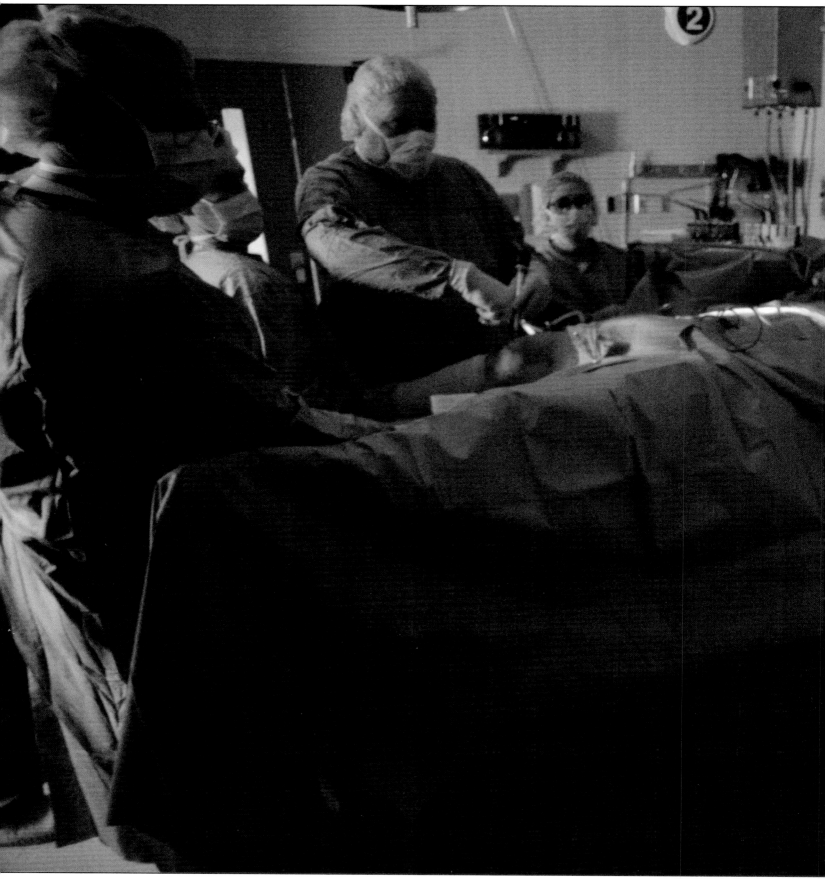

Dr. William Allen conducts arthroscopic knee surgery at the University Hospital and Clinics.

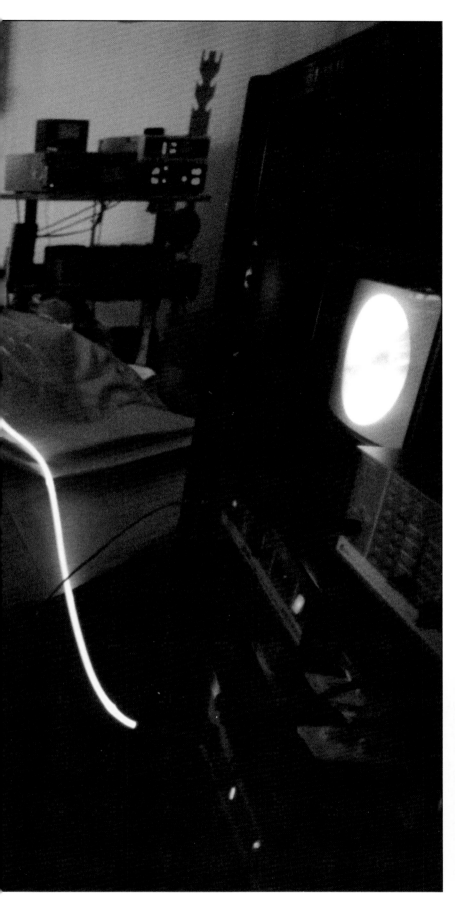

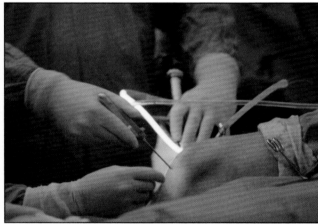

Former Mizzou football coach and athletic director, Don Faurot

Harold "Spider" Burke, class of '54, is a perennial cheerleader.

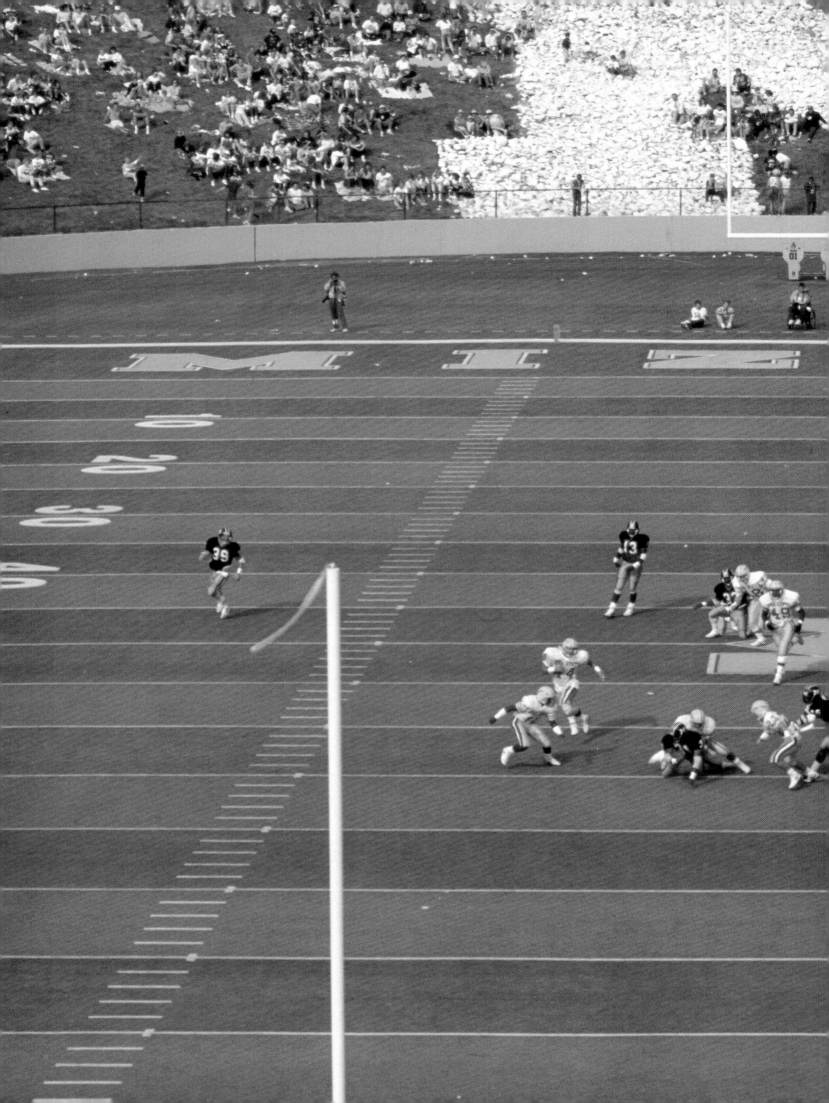

Provost Lois DeFleur

Honorary degree recipient, Lucille Bluford

Honorary degree recipient, Avis Tucker

© 1988, MATT CAMPBELL

LIKE ACADEMIC HALL, which sheltered scholars through MIZZOU's formative years, The Shack and many of the other haunts of our college crowd have been reduced to ashes or crumbling dust in the days since we were here. Bearing witness on the following pages to the vigor of those days and to the universality of the student experience, are photographs—some from a hundred and more years ago—selected from the University of Missouri Archives and the Missouri State Historical Society.

These images show us at our most somber and silly, in glory and disgrace, both proud and irreverent. Within their frames each former engineer, farmer or journalist may discover himself or herself, whether or not the likeness staring back is his or her own.

MU's first building, Academic Hall, caught fire on Saturday evening, January 9, 1892, probably as a result of faulty electrical wiring. Although students, faculty and Columbia residents fought to rescue books, paintings and furniture, much was lost in the blaze. The six Ionic columns, which are now situated at the center of Francis Quadrangle, were all that was left standing after the walls and rubble were covered over or carted away.

MISSOURI STATE HISTORICAL SOCIETY

In the years following the fire MU's columns have undergone some significant repairs. In 1937, loose pieces were removed and weatherproofing was applied to inhibit deterioration. The 1949 restoration pictured here included chipping away old and decaying bases and constructing new reinforced pedestals.

MISSOURI STATE HISTORICAL SOCIETY

Don Faurot, football coach and athletic director
from 1934 to 1956, worked with Tigers captain Clair Houston in 1936.

In 1913, Mizzou beat Rolla 44-14.

Women students from the University turned out for Homecoming in 1921.

Rolla 14

Members of the 1913 track and field squad practice pole vaulting.

The 1914 MIZZOU women's basketball team.

A common activity during freshman hazing was forcing lowly freshmen to praise the exalted sophomores, 1914.

In another freshman hazing stunt, the young male students were made to go through mock proposals with female students, 1912.

Students turned out in large numbers for Bag Rush in 1908 as Grover Kinzy made Mizzou history as the fastest freshman to shinny to the top of the flag pole.

This group of St. Louis women took part in the dance of spring at the annual Spring Follies in 1914.

Coed drill team, 1880.

MU students staged frequent stunts, festivals and parades around the turn of the century. In 1919, these young women rode the peach float in the Farmers' Fair parade.

Agriculture students posed as cowboys at a mock saloon booth during the annual Farmers' Fair, ca. 1919.

An entomology class in the 1920s.

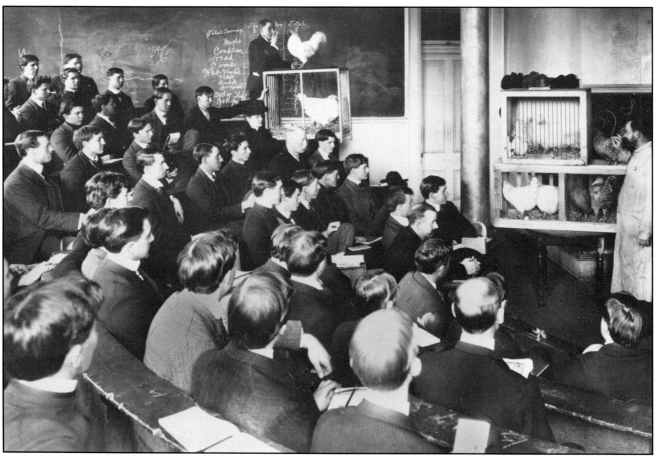

A class in poultry management in the early 1900s.

The newsroom of the 1928 *Columbia Missourian,* in what is currently the Journalism School's student lounge in Neff Hall.

A 1915 class in the Law School works on a practice trial. Established in 1867, the Law School began preparing Missouri lawyers in 1872.

MISSOURI STATE HISTORICAL SOCIETY

During the 1921 Farmers' Week, students placed signs atop the columns during the night. The letters had to be removed the next day by steeplejacks.

UNIVERSITY OF MISSOURI ARCHIVES

Engineering students celebrated St. Patrick's Day in an activity called "escorting the Blarney Stone," 1908.

MISSOURI STATE HISTORICAL SOCIETY

Hinkson Creek was a major source of entertainment for students, ca. 1908.

A YMCA-YWCA social gathering in 1913.

ALLEN AUDITORIUM
Edward A. Allen, Early Boone County resident

BAKER-PARK HALL
Sam Aaron Baker, Governor & Guy Brasfield Park, Governor

BINGHAM HALL
George Caleb Bingham, Artist, Professor and Legislator

BLAIR HALL
James T. Blair, Jr., Governor of Missouri

BRADY COMMONS,
Thomas Allen Brady, MU Vice President and Professor of History

BREWER FIELDHOUSE
Chester L. Brewer, Director of Athletics

BROOKFIELD ATHLETIC FACILITY
Dutton Brookfield, Member of Athletic Board

CAMPBELL-HARRISON HALL
Florence Harrison and Mabel Campbell, both Chairs of Home Economics

CLARK HALL
William Rogers Clark, Explorer

CONLEY HOUSE
Sanford F. Conley, Builder

CONNAWAY HALL
John Waldo Connaway, Professor of Veterinary Medicine

CRAMER HALL
Floyd Bruce Cramer, Student of Law, Died in Spanish-American War

CROWDER HALL
General Enoch Crowder, Professor of Military Science

CURTIS HALL
Winterton C. Curtis, Professor of Zoology

DEFOE HALL
Luther M. "Daddy" Defoe, Professor Emeritus of Math

DOBBS HALL
Ella Victoria Dobbs, Teacher at MU College of Education

DOCKERY-FOLK HALL
Alexander Monroe Dockery, Governor & Joseph Wingate Folk, Governor

DONNELLY HALL
Phil M. Donnelly, Governor of Missouri

ECKLES HALL
C. H. Eckles, Chairman of Dept. of Dairy Husbandry

ELLIS LIBRARY & AUDITORIUM
Elmer Ellis, MU President

FAUROT FIELD
Don Faurot, Coach, Athletic Director

GANNETT HALL
Gannett Newspaper Foundation

GARDNER-HYDE HALL
Frederick Dozier Gardner, Governor & Arthur Mastick Hyde, Governor

GENTRY HALL
Sarah Gentry, Second Woman Graduate of Full Univ. Course

GILLET HALL
Mary Louise Gillet, First Women Graduate of Normal Course

GRAHAM HALL
Robert McGhee Graham, Student of Agriculture, Died in World War II

A.P. GREEN CHAPEL
Allen P. Green, Graduate of School of Mines and Metallurgy

A.L. GUSTIN GOLF COURSE
Albert L. Gustin, Philanthropist

GWYNN HALL
Mrs. Louise Hunter Gwynn, Daughter of one of Missouri's Founding Families

HADLEY-MAJOR HALL
Herbert Spencer Hadley, Governor & Elliott Woolfolk Major, Governor

HATCH HALL
William Henry Hatch, Sponsored Hatch Act of 1887

HEARNES MULTIPURPOSE BUILDING
Warren Hearnes, Missouri Governor 1964-1972

HILL HALL
A. Ross Hill, MU President

HUDSON HALL
William Wilson Hudson, MU President and First Professor of Math

JESSE HALL
Richard Henry Jesse, MU President

JOHNSTON HALL
Eva Johnston, Teacher, Counselor, Professor Emeritus of Latin, Dean of Women

JONES HALL
John Carleton Jones, Professor of Latin, Dean of Arts and Science, MU President

KELLER AUDITORIUM
Walter D. Keller, Professor Emeritus

KUHLMAN COURT
August Kuhlman, Assistant Professor of Sociology & Katherine Kuhlman, wife

LATHROP HALL
John Hiram Lathrop First MU President

LAWS HALL
Samuel Spahr Laws, MU President

LEFEVRE HALL
Dr. George LeFevre, Professor of Zoology

LOEB HALL
Isidor Loeb, Dean of Business and Public Administration

LOWRY HALL
Benjamin Franklin Lowry & Elizabeth Lowry, sister

MCALESTER HALL
Dr. Andrew W. McAlester, Dean of Medicine

MCDAVID HALL
Frank Mitchell McDavid, Member, Board of Curators

MCHANEY HALL (RUSK REHABILITA-TION CENTER)
Powell Bassett McHaney, Pres. of Board of Curators & Howard L. Rusk, Father of Rehabilitation Medicine in U. S.

MCKEE GYMNASIUM
Mary R. McKee, Professor of Physical Education

MCREYNOLDS HALL
Allen McReynolds, Member of Board of Curators and Senator

MIDDLEBUSH HALL
Dr. Frederick A. Middlebush, MU President

MONK DRIVE
Albert H. Monk, First Veterans Hospital Administrator

MUMFORD HALL
F.B. Mumford, Dean of Agriculture

NEFF HALL
Jay Neff, Kansas City Journalist

NOYES HALL
Guy Lincoln Noyes, Dean of Medicine

PARKER HALL
William L. Parker, Philanthropist

PERSHING HALL
John Joseph Pershing, General of Armies of U.S.

PICKARD HALL
Dr. John Pickard, Founded Dept. of Art and Archaeology

READ HALL
Daniel Read, Professor, MU President. Opened MU to women.

ROLLINS HALL
Major James S. Rollins, A Founder of MU, Member of Board of Cura-tors, President Board of Curators 1870-1886

ROTHWELL GYM
Gideon F. Rothwell, President of Board of Curators

SANBORN FIELD
J. W. Sanborn, Dean and Director of College of Agriculture

SCHLUNDT HALL
Herman Schlundt, Professor of Chemistry

SCHURZ HALL
Carl Schurz, U.S. Senator from Missouri

SCHWEITZER HALL
Paul Schweitzer, Professor, First Fulltime Profes-sor of Chemistry 1894-1907, Chairman of Agriculture and Chemistry

SIMMONS FIELD
John C. Simmons, Baseball Coach

SMITH HALL
Forest Smith, Governor of Missouri

STAFFORD HALL
Richard Yearer Stafford, Student of Science and Business Admini-stration, died in World War II

STANLEY HALL
Dr. Louise Stanley, Dean of Home Economics

STEPHENS HALL
E. Sydney Stephens, Professor

STEWART HALL
Oliver M. Stewart, Chairman of Physics

SWALLOW HALL
George Clinton Swallow, Dean of Agriculture, First State Geologist of Missouri

SWITZLER HALL
William F. Switzler, Publisher of Missouri Statesman, Member of Board of Curators

TATE HALL
Lee H. Tate, Graduate of Law School

HARRY S. TRUMAN HOSPITAL
Harry S. Truman, President of the United States

TUCKER HALL
C. Mitchell Tucker, Professor and Chair of Botany

WALTER WILLIAMS HALL
Walter Williams, Founder and First Dean of Journal-ism School, MU President

WATSON PLACE
Barry Allen Watson, M.D.

WHITTEN HALL
J. C. Whitten, Professor of Agriculture

WOLPERS HALL
John H. Wolpers, President of Board of Curators